A PORTRAIT
OF
SOUTHERN WRITERS

PHOTOGRAPHS BY CURT RICHTER

FOREWORD **ROBERT COLES** | **ANN BEATTIE** AFTERWORD

HILL STREET PRESS **d** ATHENS, GEORGIA

A HILL STREET PRESS BOOK

Published in the United States of America
by Hill Street Press LLC
191 East Broad Street, Suite 209
Athens, Georgia 30601-2848 USA
706-613-7200
info@hillstreetpress.com
www.hillstreetpress.com

Printed in Spain.

Library of Congress Cataloging-in-Publication Data

Richter, Curt, 1956-
A portrait of Southern writers / photographs by Curt Richter ;
foreword by Robert Coles ; afterword by Anne Beattie.
p.   cm.
ISBN 1-892514-83-4
1. Authors, American—Southern States—Portraits. 2. Authors, American—20th century—Portraits.
3. Portrait photography—Southern States. I. Title.
PS261 .R42 2000
810.9'975'0904—dc21   00-057233

10 9 8 7 6 5 4 3 2 1

First printing

A Portrait of Southern Writers
has been designed by Anne Richmond Boston. Typeset in Adobe Officina.
The book was printed on acid-free 110LB. Acondasilk and
bound by Book Print, Barcelona, Spain.

FOREWORD

The photographs that appear in the pages ahead, in their substantial sum, once again make us wonder why a particular region of the United States has been so blessed with talented writers. Two major explanations are by now familiar, so often have they been offered: a rural storytelling tradition, and the experience of military defeat, a subsequent marginality, vulnerability, all of which prompted moral reflection, explanatory narration. No question, Southern communities, even today in a culture at the mercy of universally present television sets, manage to persist as scenes of social awareness and exchange, places where people pay one another regard, give shared expression to what has been seen and heard. When I first came to the South, in 1958, as an Air Force physician stationed in Biloxi, Mississippi, I remember being struck by the constant conversation taking place in the supermarket I frequented. People were often stopping to chat, not all of them being friends or acquaintances; and yes, despite the mighty and forbidding presence of segregation, black and white folks there (or at the post office, the gas station, the hardware store, the druggist's) found time, and had the inclination to speak to one another, say something about the weather, but not rarely go beyond that subject to matters of local interest—an accident that occurred, a road detour that had been established, with all its consequences, the sudden death of a preacher, a political figure, or yes, a known nearby no-count who, all boozed up, had lost control of his speeding car and run smack-dab into a tree while attempting to make that curve on the country road. For me, used to the silent efficiency of New England shoppers, this was an entirely

new world. I'd drive home with remembered stories in my mind rather than thoughts about what I would be doing next.

Not that the racial divide that I came to know back then wasn't a huge presence, no matter the conversational ease that seemed to prevail under certain circumstances, and therein an American story, full of social, cultural, political, moral implications—and over generations, a story that became grist for the newspapers and magazines, for Sunday sermons and court house speeches, and these days, for radio reports, television coverage, the movies. For a long time the South was a nation within a nation, its people Americans, yet apart and distinct in a vivid, daily way that centered on appearance: race as a focus for the eyes, and for the mind's response to what those eyes absorb. Put differently, race provided a constant drama in a regional life, evidence aplenty for the arbitrariness, the fatefulness of things. The grandmother of one of the black children I came to know when I observed and studied the course of school desegregation in New Orleans during the early 1960s (speaking of the way racial issues can envelop the life of a people, even the life of a temporary visitor) said to me once: "All day you have to watch your step if you're a negro, and if you're white too. There's this you should do, and there's that you shouldn't, mustn't do. You can't help but wondering about how it all came to be like it is, and why, and you think, God had something in mind, or if He didn't, then it's all crazy, and how will we ever be free of it."

The more I heard her speak, the more I'd think of passages in Faulkner—but, of course, he had heard people speak as she did, and himself had been given a moral pause similar to hers. That is what tragedy, injustice, bad luck, can do—prompt a good deal of introspection, and with it, the effort to make whatever possible sense out of what seems to be the senselessness of chance and circumstance.

When Walker Percy was asked his explanation for the South's abundance of writers, he replied with characteristically pointed terseness: "Because we lost the war"—his way of stressing the connection between suffering, pain, ignominy and the reparative efforts of the human mind, through words and more words, through storytelling which (from the Bible through Homer and Vergil to the poets and novelists of the twentieth century) has been our demonstrated human responsive inclination. "I get to thinking about what she's going through," that grandmother once said to me, referring to the child's struggle, against fierce mob opposition, to enter a boycotted elementary school—and then what she did with those thoughts: "I'll talk with my minister, and I'll talk with my daughter (the child's mother) and we'll remember what Moses went through, and Jesus, all His troubles, and we figure if it could happen to them, bad things, it can happen to us, and there's a reason, and like our minister says, we have to show the world the truth, through what we do and say, that's our job in this long story."

She had a little schooling, but that last word showed a perspective not always available to the best-educated minds—a realization that in life, as in art, individuals engage with one another, shape one another's lives, are protagonists or antagonists, are caught up in one or another unfolding set of circumstances, even dramatic actions of various kinds. She and her family, especially her granddaughter, were contributors and recipients of a kind of moral energy that has been the South's legacy—the redemptive side to a long chronicle of racially connected fear and hate. So many of the region's writers, Faulkner foremost, of course, but dozens of others who appear here on these pages, or who died before these pictures were taken are men and women who have wrested "art" from the "life" that they share with others who call Dixie home.

To look at these pictures is to struggle with the inevitable mystery of talent, if not genius—appearances will tell us only so much, and certainly not give us the clues we yearn to possess as to what makes for, accounts for, in Henry James's phrase, "the madness of art." Yet, we want ever so much to connect to a person's presence, his or her self-presentation, with the stories or poems or essays or plays we have read, and here, for those of us interested in a region's imposing collective cultural legacy, are those particular portraits. Here are individuals standing strong and self-assured, or in seeming frailty, vulnerability. Here are individuals in wheel chairs, down but far from out. Here are eyes—some of them looking up, some down, some aimed at a scene the nature of which the viewers can only guess. Here are hands folded, or arms hanging loose. Here are, on occasion, a spouse, a child—and yes, in one instance, a snake; in another, some eggs. Here are heads bare, or covered, heads tilted or held ever so erect, so as to oblige the camera's lens. Here is informality and gentility and propriety—a mix of the casual and the ever so correct. Here are young and old—we know some of these writers have a long and promising time ahead, and we know some are close to death as they faced a patient, determined, tactful, and respectful photographer who sought them out, it can be said, in the nick of time. Here are writers become icons of our era, so that no picture, however thoughtfully composed, taken, can rescue them from familiarity to us (a mixed blessing, of course, because lost in such a certainty of knowledge—oh yes, I recognize him, her!—are dozens of important private, personal truths that never see the light of day).

So it goes. So they all sit and stand for us, a camera's attention become our many human sights to consider: a broad range of late twentieth-century writing folk of Southern background—in the words of the Book of Common Prayer,

A
PORTRAIT
OF
SOUTHERN
WRITERS

"all sorts and conditions." Surely, in some instances, we are right to note the neckties or the lack of them, the buttoned-down elegance or the bold, even defiant irreverence, or the proclamation of irregularity that has been conveyed. How all those postures and poses, those efforts to insist or reveal or hide, connect with the work that has prompted inclusion in this book—that is for each of us to consider as we turn these pages. Inevitably, we will try to link in some way a caught second of a lived life, as it is presented here, with the published consequences of days, years, given to the pen, the typewriter, the computer. "I go about my plodding life as best I can," the New Jersey poet and physician William Carlos Williams once remarked, and then he added this exception of sorts to that daily experience: "But when I'm in that study with the typewriter, I shed my skin—it's a leap into another life, and I can stay there only so long." I remembered those words, of course, when I saw the snake in one of the pictures; but I also kept thinking of those words as I went, so to speak, from writer to writer in the pages ahead—a visit to their ordinary lives, and a reminder ironically, that it is in the other life, to which they occasionally or persistently or eagerly or reluctantly "leap," that they achieve the statements that make us want to visit with them here visually, even as we remember with gratitude and respect our visits with them as their readers.

Robert Coles

Cambridge, Massachusetts

October 1996

PREFACE

LIGHT IS A THING

It is over ten years ago that I photographed Eudora Welty and this project began. Several months before my meeting Ms. Welty, I had met another Southern writer, Louis Rubin. A magazine in New York had flown me down to Chapel Hill, North Carolina to photograph him for a story about his press, Algonquin. Louis had not seen any of my work, but that afternoon he commissioned me to photograph the portraits of the founding members of the Fellowship of Southern Writers for their archives at the University of Tennessee at Chattanooga. There were twenty-eight members, and it took two years to get them, one by one, in front of my camera. It was suggested to me that I expand the project into a book, so I did. I anticipated it would take several months to complete the project, instead it took six years.

Once I had compiled a list of contemporary Southern writers, it was difficult to find out how to reach them. I found the answer at the New York City Forty-Second Street Library where there is a room dedicated to contemporary literature. I started at *A*. For the sake of the writers' privacy I won't reveal exactly how I found their home addresses, but it was with the library's computer. The best source for contacting the writers turned out to be the writers themselves. In the beginning, every writer I photographed gave me the names and addresses of three others. Once I started the portraits it was hard to know when to stop. Near the end, I photographed George Garrett, a writer with the reputation of knowing everyone. With some reluctance on having my load increased, I asked George if he would look at my list to see if there was anyone I'd missed. Indeed he did give me the names of two more writers, but I knew I'd

A
PORTRAIT
OF
SOUTHERN
WRITERS

done a good job when he asked: "Do you mind if I write down some of these addresses? There are several writers here I'd like to contact." Some writers declined being photographed for this book, but not many. A few I was never able to locate. To the viewer of this book, I apologize if there is a face missing, it is probably because I failed with my camera and lights. The last portrait was of Alice Walker—a brief encounter in a side room of a hotel lobby in Chapel Hill. The photography project ended a short walk from where it began and with thousands of miles and hours in between.

The writers were remarkably generous with their time and they were open with their ideas and willing to listen to mine. What a writer does with ink and paper is quite different from what I do with camera and film. Thinking about our given means of expression engaged me while traveling from one state line to the next, but we both make objects. I talked with many of them about our different mediums, the structure of forms, and what one hopes to achieve in making them and trying to make them with beauty. *Light is a thing.* It is a particle of energy moving at the fastest speed possible in our universe. For a photographer light is essential, a photograph cannot be made without it. In a different way, light is a thing to a writer as well, but perhaps for them, so is sound.

"A photograph is always sentimental, because it is always about the past," Max Steele declared on our enjoyable day together. My response was to ask him if he felt sentimental about the photograph of the suspected Vietcong spy with a revolver pointed at his head. "Lord no, of course not." If there was an exception, then Max's statement could not be true, but there are many truths. Most of my life has been spent looking at the world as a photographer. The answers to many questions I feel I have found; but many questions remain, and probably even more have yet to be discovered. Malcolm X remarked that he did not trust a man who did

not wear a watch because it indicated he had no respect for time. Time, for him, was the ultimate measure of success or failure. A photograph is a document of light and time. Painters and photographers move through space with one eye closed, eventually coming to rest at a singular point of perception. "Think of what one can do with a book, you can take any number of characters through time and place. Form the events of their lives and their evolving natures. To be able to reveal their thoughts and emotions and all with something you can hold in your hand," William Faulkner told his students. A writer's tools are twenty-six characters, each letter representing a sound. Depending on the language, the letters are placed together to make different words. Each word a metaphor for an idea, real or abstract. A book is a string of words put together in a particular order to tell a story. In writing a novel, the author creates a myriad of perspectives, and, hopefully, with the possibility that the reader will be able to find many of their own.

When I asked Andrew Lytle why the South had such a strong heritage of literature it was clear from his response that this was a question he had long considered. "In order to create anything original, one has to accept the possibility of failure. When we lost the Civil War, failure became a part of the South's culture." The difference between a writer's palette and mine was made clear by Mary Hood. At the end of an afternoon of talk and iced tea, she rose from her rocking chair as I was about to depart. "This chair belonged to my grandmother," she said as she turned to look back at it. "And my grandmother would never take a seat in the chair without first moving it, even if just a little." Driving back to Atlanta that day, I thought about the image Mary had placed in my head. One could spend a lifetime living with someone and not see what she had seen, or at least not be able to talk about it. Her grandmother's slight adjustments were her way to reclaim the chair, but it took a writer's vision to see it.

The only tangible evidence of my Guggenheim Fellowship is my car. Four wheels, and a pile of prints and an even bigger pile of negatives. On the last leg of my final journey South for this book, the odometer in my car rolled over. All those nines became all those zeros. It happened somewhere on the Maryland Turnpike and, several days later, I realized it must have been near the Mason-Dixon Line. There were so many roads I traveled so many times. My favorite is Highway 319, a two lane black top that links Tifton, Georgia to Tallahassee, Florida. The first time I drove it was when I applied to graduate school at Florida State University. Since then, I have driven it more times than I can count and always alone. There are strip malls with restaurant chains along the way but mostly the road passes through flat farmland and a few small towns that appear to have lost their purpose. It has always given me pleasure to drive it, even at night. I cannot say why I love it, but I do. The poet, John Stone, told me Seamus Heaney believed "it" was the most powerful word in the English language. Auguste Renoir said that what makes a work of art great is an intangible *it*.

New York City will always be my home, but as I sit at my desk and look out at the rooftops of Helsinki, I wonder if I'll ever live there again. I'm reminded of my return to my studio from my longest trip to the South taking portraits. There, waiting for me, was a pile of mail two feet high. Most of it was junk but on top was a plain, white index card from Donald Justice. A brief note to say he would sit for me, but he thought I should know he no longer considered himself a Southerner, even though he was born there. His note ended: "and now, just now, I'm staring out the study window at the snow and ice, and not minding it at all."

Curt Richter

Helsinki, Finland

June 2000

Dedicated to Louis D. Rubin Jr.

LOUIS D. RUBIN JR.

Autumn 1988

Chapel Hill, North Carolina

HUNT HAWKINS & DAUGHTER

Spring 1995

Tallahassee, Florida

ALICE WALKER

Autumn 1996

Chapel Hill, North Carolina

WILLIAM STYRON

Spring 1989

New York City

REYNOLDS PRICE

Winter 1989

Chapel Hill, North Carolina

WILLIAM BALDWIN

Winter 1995

McClellanville, South Carolina

RITA MAE BROWN

Spring 1995

Afton, Virginia

JOSEPHINE HUMPHREYS

Winter 1995

Charleston, South Carolina

ISHMAEL REED

Winter 1996

New York City

WILL D. CAMPBELL

Autumn 1994

Mount Juliet, Tennessee

BETH HENLEY

Winter 1995

New York City

ANDREW LYTLE

Winter 1989

Monteagle, Tennessee

SHEILA BOSWORTH

Spring 1995

Covington, Louisiana

KAYE GIBBONS

Winter 1995

Raleigh, North Carolina

EUDORA WELTY

Winter 1989

Jackson, Mississippi

RICHARD FORD

Spring 1995

New Orleans, Louisiana

LISA ALTHER

Summer 1995

Shelburne, Vermont

LARRY L. KING

Spring 1995

Washington, D.C.

MARY HOOD

Autumn 1995

Woodstock, Georgia

PAT CONROY

Winter 1995

New York City

DENNIS & VICKI COVINGTON

Spring 1995

Birmingham, Alabama

DORIS BETTS

Summer 1994

Chapel Hill, North Carolina

JIM GRIMSLEY

Autumn 1995

Atlanta, Georgia

DONALD JUSTICE

Autumn 1995

New York City

GUY DAVENPORT

Autumn 1994

Lexington, Kentucky

MARK RICHARD

Spring 1995

Oxford, Mississippi

WILLIE MORRIS

Spring 1995

Jackson, Mississippi

DAVID BOTTOMS

Winter 1995

Marietta, Georgia

MADISON JONES

Winter 1995

Auburn, Alabama

SHELBY FOOTE

Summer 1995

Memphis, Tennessee

JAYNE ANNE PHILLIPS

Summer 1995

Newton, Massachusetts

CLEANTH BROOKS

Winter 1989

Fairfield, Connecticut

ROBERT PENN WARREN

Winter 1989

Fairfield, Connecticut

WINSTON GROOM

Spring 1995

Point Clear, Alabama

ROBERT MORGAN

Summer 1995

Freeville, New York

JIMMY CARTER

Autumn 1995

Atlanta, Georgia

BAILEY WHITE

Winter 1995

Thomasville, Georgia

LEE SMITH

Autumn 1994

Chapel Hill, North Carolina

BARRY HANNAH

Spring 1995

Oxford, Mississippi

BERTHA HARRIS

Summer 1995

Adamsville, Rhode Island

HORTON FOOTE

Autumn 1995

Boston, Massachusetts

SARAH GILBERT

Winter 1995

Winnsboro, South Carolina

WILLIAM PRICE FOX

Winter 1995

Winnsboro, South Carolina

JOHN STONE

Winter 1995

Tucker, Georgia

DONNA TARTT

Winter 1996

New York City

ANN BEATTIE

Summer 1995

York, Maine

JAMES WHITEHEAD

Summer 1995

Fayetteville, Arkansas

RALPH ELLISON

Autumn 1990

New York City

WENDELL BERRY

Spring 1991

Chattanooga, Tennessee

T. R. PEARSON

Autumn 1992

Brooklyn, New York

BOB SHACOCHIS

Autumn 1995

Tallahassee, Florida

VALERIE SAYERS

Summer 1995

New York City

ANNE RIVERS SIDDONS

Winter 1995

Atlanta, Georgia

JOHN EGERTON

Autumn 1994

Nashville, Tennessee

EUGENE WALTER

Spring 1995

Mobile, Alabama

FRED CHAPPELL

Summer 1990

Greensboro, North Carolina

PERCIVAL EVERETT

Summer 1995

Philadelphia, Pennsylvania

JOHN HOPE FRANKLIN

Summer 1990

Raleigh, North Carolina

CONNIE CULPEPPER

Spring 1995

Nashville, Tennessee

JONATHAN WILLIAMS

Autumn 1994

Highlands, North Carolina

GEORGE GARRETT

Summer 1995

Charlottesville, Virginia

C. VANN WOODWARD

Winter 1989

Fairfield, Connecticut

BOBBIE ANN MASON

Winter 1996

Ithaca, New York

ALLAN GURGANUS

Winter 1995

Hillsborough, North Carolina

DAPHNE ATHAS

Autumn 1994

Chapel Hill, North Carolina

VICTOR NUNEZ

Spring 1995

Tallahassee, Florida

ANDRE DUBUS

Summer 1995

Haverhill, Massachusetts

JESSE HILL FORD

Autumn 1995

Nashville, Tennessee

M.A. HARPER

Winter 1995

North Charleston, South Carolina

ANN PATCHETT

Spring 1995

Nashville, Tennessee

CHARLES WRIGHT

Winter 1993

Charlottesville, Virginia

ROMULUS LINNEY

Winter 1993

New York City

ALBERT MURRAY

Autumn 1994

New York City

GAIL GODWIN

Spring 1995

Woodstock, New York

DAVE SMITH

Spring 1995

Baton Rouge, Louisiana

HENRY TAYLOR

Autumn 1995

Lincoln, Virginia

PADGETT POWELL

Winter 1995

Gainesville, Georgia

MILLER WILLIAMS

Winter 1995

Fayetteville, Arkansas

BRENT WADE

Summer 1995

Gambrills, Maryland

JAMES DICKEY

Summer 1994

Columbia, South Carolina

TINA MCELROY ANSA

Winter 1995

St. Simons Island, Georgia

LARRY BROWN

Winter 1995

Oxford, Mississippi

PAUL HEMPHILL

Autumn 1994

Atlanta, Georgia

WILLIAM HOFFMAN

Spring 1995

Charlottesville, Virginia

ELIZABETH DEWBERRY

Spring 1995

Nashville, Tennessee

ROBERT OLEN BUTLER

Spring 1995

Nashville, Tennessee

A. R. AMMONS

Spring 1989

Ithaca, New York

DORI SANDERS

Winter 1995

Charlotte, North Carolina

TERRY KAY

Winter 1995

Lilburn, Georgia

BRET LOTT

Winter 1995

Charleston, South Carolina

CATHRYN HANKLA

Autumn 1995

Troutville, Virginia

HARRY CREWS

Spring 1995

Gainesville, Florida

WALKER PERCY

Winter 1989

Covington, Louisiana

ROBERT BAUSCH

Autumn 1995

Broad Run, Virginia

RICHARD BAUSCH

Spring 1995

Broad Run, Virginia

AFTERWORD

Where a writer lives is almost always one of the two facts you can count on learning from reading the author's bio on the back flap of her book. The other is what my grandmother would have called "her circumstances"—meaning, with whom she lives, and whether or not there are children. In contemporary bios, cats and dogs are sometimes interchangeable with children, so that we read: "Writer X lives in Jackson, Mississippi with her husband and two dalmations." The assumption is that the writer is rooted in that place, but anyone who knows writers knows that they are vagabonds. Sometimes they live where they live because of a teaching job. Other times, it's because their mate has roots in that area. But more often, they're just passing through, whether or not they know it. In my own case, only two or three times have I still been living where my newly published book has placed me. Writers move around a lot. This sometimes has to do with research, but more often it's a kind of exploration of ones-self, an experiment to see what you're like under different circumstances. A resistance against being situated in one place is analogous to what writers try to infuse into their work: If you don't keep moving, the writing will become de-energized, and repetitive writing is doomed.

I realize that many writers have spent all, or most of their lives in or around the same place, though that isn't usual in America. When we think of Eudora Welty, the first thing that comes to mind may be the P.O., but then immediately thereafter we think of Jackson, Mississippi. Others have migrated, and some of those have formed expatriate communities, but within those communities, they seem to be identified as Southern writers. Editors compiling anthologies will track down a

Southern writer in Alaska or Prague, because it is assumed the Southern writer trails his or her Southernness like clouds of glory. There are, of course, those who have returned to the South after spending long periods elsewhere, such as Charles Wright.

Wherever they go, one of the things that inevitably accompanies them is the watchfulness of others, who see them all as representatives; in them resides a literary tradition, a still not quite defined otherness as formidable as it is mysterious.

Flannery O'Connor, in a lecture given at Georgetown University, said: "The South is traditionally hostile to outsiders, except on her own terms. She is traditionally against intruders, foreigners from Chicago or New Jersey, all those who come from afar with moral energy that increases in direct proportion to the distance from home. It is difficult to separate the virtues of this quality from the narrowness which accompanies and colors it for the outside world. It is more difficult still to reconcile the South's instinct to preserve her identity with her equal instinct to fall eager victim to every poisonous breath from Hollywood or Madison Avenue. But good and evil appear to be joined in every culture at the spine, and as far as the creation of a body of fiction is concerned, the social is superior to the purely personal. Somewhere is better than anywhere. And traditional manners, however unbalanced, are better than no manners at all." (What O'Connor called "the purely personal" has become a mass *mea culpa* of memoir writing that I suspect would not much interest her; certainly the entire concept of manners has been through so many permutations from the time and context in which she wrote that Miss Manners herself would have a difficult task explaining to O'Connor why manners so quickly became a lost art. But I digress.) Ask people what they think of when you say, "Southern writer," and my guess is that many will not immediately come up with a generalization about them, but about the region, itself—much like O'Connor's explanation of the South in her essay. But then (here they

may hesitate) as for the *writers,* aren't there those certain, you know, grotesque elements . . . because, I mean, those Southern writers can just be so *crazy!* Southern writers are expected to be rooted in their region. They are expected to be highly imaginative (this is the euphemism for crazy, which people make as a generalization about all writers). They are expected to have a strange sense of humor. Their characters are expected to have a lot to say. Though these characterizations are hardly limited to writers from the South, I think there is still a pervasive belief that Southern writers are telling real stories disguised as fiction, which they can learn about just by being in the right place at the right time—all of the South being the right place. I mention these common stereotypes not merely to dismiss them, but to put forth the idea that Southern writers, in being made conveniently larger than life, in being romanticized until they are a little scarier than others of their kind, have come to typify the extreme of the species: they're more flamboyant, wilder—they're the leopards that make us nervous around cats, the fall guys for writers in general.

Curt Richter came to my house in Maine one day when a friend—a Southern writer, as it happens—was visiting from Texas. She and my husband decided to go sailing, running off before they'd have to make pleasantries with the day's visitor, rubbing it in that I was stuck with an obligation. Being as unrepresentative a Northerner as a Southerner, I hate sailing, so I waved them off with equanimity. My mixed emotions only had to do with being photographed. Of course, everyone worries about what they will look like in a photograph. The worry is not only that you might not look good, but you might not be able to tell whether you look good or not. "What do you think of this?" I'd said many times over the years, to my husband or to friends, holding out a photograph that did not please or displease so much as it

perplexed me. The worry is, of course, that they will not really level with you about how you look. Alternatively, they might really level with you ("Oh—look at those charming little worry lines at the sides of your eyes!"). Since one of my best friends was a photographer, I often hear his words before a shoot begins: "Annie—light on the make-up" (He would make his words light when he said this). "And chin up. Chin up" (I see him with his tipped-up chin). I put on a gauzy skirt I rarely wore (hedging my bets: If I looked silly, at least it wasn't me in the photograph) and a weird ring I did sometimes wear, just because it was so ludicrous that it was amusing to hear what people would say. We hadn't finished furnishing the house in 1995, but we did have an Empire sofa that I loved. In fact, Curt took a picture of me on the sofa, gauzy skirt spread around me, big ring pointed at the camera like a piece of kryptonite, and I'm not just saying this: *in the photograph, the sofa looks great.* In the photograph included in this book, you will note that the sofa does not appear.

As an observer of this collection of photographs, as distinct from being the subject of one of them, I can make a number of observations. I know some of the writers—not the majority, but some—and with those faces that were familiar, I could hardly take my eyes away. Perhaps they would have the same reaction, looking at me . . . trying to discover *what?* Whether the expression was quintessential (I'd probably be the last to know), or a revelation; how much vitality made it from the person into the photograph; what aspects seem to have been revealed unconsciously. It's also interesting to study the composition and to consider the question of the person's placement within the parameters—how this structuring might also reveal something about the subject. The backgrounds are uniformly obliterated or so unobtrusive as to almost disappear, though Richter, unlike Avedon in *The American West,* is clearly not there to document. Some of the images verge on being formal

portraits—something Karsh might have done. But with Karsh, you would expect more
. . . straightforwardness, for lack of a better word. When you have anything
resembling straightforwardness here, there is some element in the expression that
undercuts the formality. Not a photograph here could be included with a curriculum
vitae, without the recipient being taken aback. Had the angle of her head been
different, Bobbie Ann Mason's photograph might have been more conventional. As it
is, the riveting asymmetry of her face, coupled with the delicate fineness of her hair,
suggests both the strong presence of the woman, as well as a certain enigmatic
delicacy. I know her as smiling and disarmingly direct. But of course: beneath that
was always this other person. That, it seems to me, is something very difficult to do
as a photographer: to wait for the expressive moment that has little or nothing to do
with the face people usually present to the world, while at the same time avoiding
the slackness of an out-take. (Avedon's legendary photograph of Marilyn Monroe, eyes
dropped, would be another classic example of succeeding in this way.)

Notice the way so many of Richter's subjects clasp their hands—the
hands that take on a life of their own when they write. Viewed apart from the whole,
seen only in detail, it would often be difficult to say whether they were restful hands
or tortured hands; only when you see the subject's face, read the subject's body
language, can you know (look at Andrew Lytle's hands; look at Kaye Gibbons's).
Reynolds Price's hands could exist apart from his photograph as a piece of sculpture;
John Coplans or Holly Wright, I'm sure, would love to move in close for a detail. It's
tempting, but ultimately unfair, here, to separate the hands from the portrait.
Reynolds's hands become the second focal point of the circle, as the eye travels from
head to hands. The constant movement of the eye becomes the animation that
counterbalances Reynolds's inwardness.

I admire Curt Richter's work not just because it's striking and unusual, but also because it's subtle. I know something about placing people (albeit, imaginary) in certain contexts—in using the external world to help explain, or reinforce, psychological portraits. Backgrounds, contexts—which, for all intents and purposes, Curt Richter does not depend upon—can do a lot of the work for a photographer. In theory, they can make the task easier, just as excessive characters are usually easier for the writer to present vividly than subtle ones. There are certain photographers whose landscapes are personified (Sally Mann's recent work), others who poeticize a landscape through portraiture (Avedon's *American West*). But it is extremely difficult to make portraits with only the sparest, simplest props. Richter is somewhat analogous to Samuel Beckett in his working method. In the arts, at the end of the millennium, there has been a drift away from O'Connor's belief that "somewhere is better than anywhere," so that we have become acclimated, if not necessarily comfortable, with the idea that simple forms can possess the greatest intensity. (Cyberspace is nowhere that is nevertheless considered a place; it is also, inevitably, a metaphor.)

Finally, what strikes me about these photographs is their candor. The subjects were comfortable with the photographer, and he with them. They're riveting, because you have to look deep within. As you do that, of course you are looking within yourself, only momentarily studying the portrait of another.

Ann Beattie

Key West, Florida

January 2000

ACKNOWLEDGMENTS

My thanks to the following foundations, organizations, colleagues, and friends for their help.

The Fellowship of Southern Writers; the John Simon Guggenheim Foundation; the John Kobal Foundation; the United States / Finland Fulbright Commission; the Italian Fulbright Commission; the United States Information Service, Finland and Germany; the Foundation Center; Poets & Writers; the National Endowment for the Humanities; Centro Studi Americani, Roma; Amerika Haus, Frankfurt; and the United States Embassy, Finland

To Jane Clark, who sent me on assignment to Chapel Hill and, inadvertently, started this project. William Nabers, who saw it as a book long before I did. John Langston and JoAnne Prichard for their early encouragement. Ann Beattie and Robert Coles for their generous contributions. Phillip duChateau for his "knee jerking" support with both the exhibition and the book. My editor, Judy Long, our chance meeting on a boat ride off the coast of Finland brought the book to publication. My wife and closest friend, Jaana Laine-Richter, who helped me finish what I had started.

Thanks also to Pasi Aaltonen, Kristoffer Albrecht, Sara Antonelli, Larry Bach, Bill and Alice Bamberger, Mary Lou Beattie, Phil Block, Anne Richmond Boston, Dot Brittingham, John Cohen, George Core, Lisa Cremin, Simon Crocker, Jed Devine, U.S. Ambassador Eric Edelman, Robert Fichter, Peter Galassi, George Garrett, Chan Gordon, Angela Grant, Jan Groover, Lois Guarino, Mark Haworth-Booth, Marvin Heiferman, Robert Hennessy, William Hufstader, Josephine Humphreys, Barry Jones,

Robert Kozma, Aaron Kurzen, Ville Kettunen, the Laine family, Jean-Claude Lemagny, Daniel Lipson, Davien Littlefield, Leila Mustanoja, Fitzer Mills, Markku and Sari Nurminen, Tom Payton, Rod and Joan Perkins and their family, Pam Roberts, Sally Robinson, Jimmy Roche, Josh Rockwell, Bill and Ann Roy and their family, Cynthia Van Roden, John Seigenthaler, Marc Smirnoff, Cork Smith, Adam and Nicole Straus, Phyllis Straus, Nancy Ulin, Jonathan Williams and Miller Williams.

And to my parents and grandparents for all they have given and shown me.

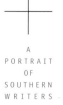